The
Heavenly
Dog Father

PRAYER BOOK

LARA MAGALLON

Heavenly Dog Father, Prayer Book

Lara Magallon

ISBN: 9781636494845

Published by Lara Magallon

Printed in the United States of America

"Aedh Wishes for the Cloths of Heaven,"
William Butler Yeats

Had I the heaven's embroidered cloths,
Enwrought with golden and silver light,
The blue and the dim and the dark cloths
Of night and light and the half light,
I would spread the cloths under your feet:
But I, being poor, have only my dreams:
I have spread my dreams under your feet:
Tread softly because you tread on my dreams.

DEDICATION

I dedicate this book to every dog and dog lover in existence. Dogs are such a precious gift--they teach us about love and what the word "love" actually represents. They never fail to love us unconditionally no matter how we treat them. A prime example is a dog that has been abandoned on the side of the road yet waits for years for their beloved master to return. Or a dog that refuses to leave their masters grave and is delivered food and water by caring people.

Dogs also provide a mirror into our lives. Educating us about who we are and what we are about at the time. They completely fill up a void within our heart and soul. A place we never thought we had. But we have had it all along. We just needed a dog to point it out.

We will never find ourselves alone when we own a dog. With their graceful face and warm paws followed by a swish of hairy ears and fur, they forever guide us through our turbulent life.

With a dog, who needs a high priced therapist? We have the very best one right in front of our eyes! I only wish dogs outlived us. That is their only flaw.

Thank you to Miss Angel Jeannette. Rex, Peanut, Shadow, Paula Stein, Michelle Magallon, Keith Furrow, Romano Quattropanetti , Jim Dovel, Conrad Herring, Jenny Sohl, Ryan and Julia Mock, Jordan and Taylor Mock, Kelly Mock, George Noujaim, Nancy Priestly, Carol Richardson, Dan and Kevin Mock, Mark Brown, Docteures Giselle , Andy Loehr, Diana Regentz, John Humphrey, Mike Murga, Angelo Pizelo, John Mills, Tom Schenck, Steve Golden, Matt DeMeyer, my spiritual communities, St Elizabeth Seton, Scripps Hospital and Body Mind And Soul.

In loving memory of Diane Street, Jeannette Dyer, Florencia Magallon, Wayne Richardson, Granny, Nala and Bandit who are in heaven watching over me. There is not one day that I do not miss your presence in my life. I pray that you and the angels guide us on our mission.

And, in loving memory of any precious "best friends" of my contributors who have crossed the rainbow bridge during the writing of the Heavenly Dog Father Prayer Book. If we are quiet we can see these beautiful souls playing ball and tag with other dogs that have since passed. They are all healthy now. You have blessed us all so much.

A special thank you…

To everyone who contributed their prayers to the "Heavenly Dog Father Prayer Book," I honor each and every one of you. Without you there would be no book. It was my intent to leave every word you contributed as it was. I didn't want to minimize your thoughts or prayers. I consider your feelings sacred; you shared a piece of your heart. I hope you will be proud of "our" book. Thank you for believing in me.

Lastly to my "friend family" and "world-wide social media dog family"… what would I do without you? Where would I be without you?

Words of Wisdom
By Reverend Keith Furrow

I'm excited to be part of this amazing journey and process that Lara Magallon is experiencing. Lara has an amazing heart for service and a passion for our furry companions, and more specifically canines. This passion is a ministry of love. Our fur babies as many call them have a special place in our lives. There are as many varieties, shapes, sizes and personalities as there are in the human family. Dogs live with us and share our lives, homes, farms, ranches, business' and families.

To me it is not by coincidence that Dog spelled backwards is God. When we look into the beautiful loving eyes of our canine partners it is very easy to see their unconditional love. They guide us, comfort us, love us, and protect us. For most of us, they help us to reach a peaceful state and to block out the clutter of life. Just petting them, touching them or picking them up immediately brings us to a state of peace and bliss.

I have had the pleasure of many great fur babies in my life. I will never forget any of them. I remember those that have made their transition and are waiting patiently for me at the other end of the metaphorical rainbow bridge as described by the great poem written by ————.

Currently my little bundle of joy is a beautiful 13 1/2 year old, 7 pound Bichon Bolognese. She is truly amazing. She has such a fantastic personality and nearly never stops kissing my wife and me. She invented what we call a triple kiss, and always insists that we three way kiss when ever one of us gets home and we are all united. She loves to travel and goes everywhere possible with us. We hardly like to go anywhere she can't attend and usually we choose to hurry home to be with her if she is not with us.

Each time one of our fur babies make their transition I'm struck by the pain of the loss, and for a moment I feel I can never do this again. Then my beautiful and loving wife reminds me that how much they added to our lives and how we were able to give them an amazing life. Even as I write this I'm holding back the tears, as I become aware that Precious Fiona Rose Leonarkis-Furrow our fur baby is getting up in years and like us will eventually make that transition. Just like every other living thing in our universe she/we are not promised tomorrow and she will some day temporarily leave us. It is said it is better to have loved and lost then to not have loved at all. This is certainly true when it comes to the love of man's/ women's best friend. The good news is that once you touch this love as in all love you experience in your heart, you can never be separated from this love. If you have not experienced the joy and love of sharing your life with a fur baby such as dog or kitty, I recommend you adopt a new family member ASAP.

Namaste'
Rev Keith Furrow

INTRODUCTION

The warmest welcome to the "Heavenly Dog Father Prayer Book" I am so glad you've chosen to join us. I became inspired to write the prayer book while my best friend and beloved family member Boomer (better known as Granny) was under going radiation.

Granny bravely met each and every treatment while I cried my eyes out until I was blinded by puffy eyes. I used to wonder what he thought about me during this ordeal. Was I a model of weakness? In human terms anyone could see I was a mess!

Did he think I had lost my mind? No doubt, Granny thought so. Gladly he was much braver than I during his courageous battle with cancer.

In the midst of all this grief and confusion, a seed was planted that blossomed into a held fast dream. I felt the urge to write a prayer book from the dog's perspective, not a human's which is so common. So why not start with Granny's prayers? So there you have it.

During the four years of battling cancer, CVS Angel Care became my second home. Even after my beloved Granny was greeted by the Heavenly Dog Father, whenever I drive by the facility I am filled with memories that envelope me in peace. A piece of my heart will remain forever there along with Granny's essence.

Dogs, even while sick or dying, attempt to appear to be healthy, when in realty they aren't. I am convinced they don't want us to worry. Their sole mission in life is to guard our soul until the very end, our ever present support system. But I ask you to consider, is there really an end to this beautiful energy called "dogs"?

Oddly enough, the same day Granny rejoined the

Heavenly Dog Father, I was blessed to witness him touching "nose to nose" with my new rescue Miss Angel Jeannette. (Named after my grandmother Jeannette D'Arcy)

Clearly and unmistakably, this was a sign from the Heavenly Dog Father that Granny was indeed passing the torch to her. It was now Miss Angel Jeannette's responsibility to guide me through life, just as Granny once did. She became my heart and soul, keeping me safe as my pinnacle of strength.

I am convinced that we all have a journey in this life, whatever that might be. Sometimes we have no idea what our path is until we find ourselves surprisingly treading upon it. And if you don't think dogs do as well, look a little closer. I am here to tell you they do. They too have a soul and exist elsewhere in the heavens above. Just look at all of the photographs of "dog shaped clouds."

There is a brilliant light that shines within each and every one of us. We just must access it.

May we attract that which we are and detract that which we are not.

May we be enlightened to find the true reason for our existence and our weaknesses instead become our strengths.

May we go forward in our infinite power! We are limitless.

And guess what?

Dogs knew this all along.

Each dog has a prayer inside of them.

"We delight in the beauty of the butterfly, but rarely admit the changes it has gone through to achieve that beauty."
—Maya Angelou

Granny Was One Of A Kind

For: Lara Magallon

Dear Heavenly Dog Father,

I am asking you to help my Mommy find the strength inside her being to deal with my cancer. We were clueless as to what the funny looking lump that suddenly appeared on my leg might be. What was it? Could it be a bee sting? I hoped so. Everyone knows how much I love playing in the yard.

I reluctantly visited Dr. Singh and he performed a biopsy. I didn't want to get out of the car. Surprisingly, the results came back confirming I had "cancer." Dr. Singh said it was the type of cancer with "octopus like tentacles" that would spread throughout my body.

Cancer, me? Was I hearing the word correctly? Surely, my biopsy results were mixed up with another dog. Mommy was silent all the way home. I didn't mean to be sick!

Heavenly Dog Father, do you know why mom's eyes were red and swollen all the time? Suddenly she started to cancel events at the last minute. Mommy never used to do that.

With your mighty powers can you make me all better? I hate letting Mommy down. Remember that coat of armor you created for dogs? Can you toss it down from heaven I need it.

Heavenly Dog Father, please circulate my prayers in heaven. If by some chance I don't get better, tell Mommy I will never leave her side.

In hopeful prayer,
Boomer (Granny)

Little Miss Angel Jeannette, The Wild One!

For: Lara Magallon

Dear Heavenly Dog Father,

Everybody knows I can't take the place of Boomer (Granny), but can't I at least try? You advised me that my new Mommy's heart was shattered into a million pieces after she lost Granny.

During his passing, you and I witnessed him running on the multi colored Rainbow Bridge with a smile and a ball set firmly in his mouth. I could tell that Boomer was thrilled to meet you Heavenly Dog Father.

I could barely catch a glimpse of him after he arrived in heaven because he was surrounded by millions of dogs playing with lots of shiny toys.

What can I possibly do to ease my new Mommy's pain? You created me with a huge heart and a really bossy personality. Most dogs are clueless about me. They take me on face value. They think I am shallow but I am far from it.

Heavenly Dog Father you saw the real Angel Jeannette. I am not as tough as I look. Actually, I am pretty fragile inside. I was desperate to find a good family who would take me.

I was skin and bones when I arrived at Mommy's house. Everyone could see my spine and count my ribs. The rescue agency was mistaken when they said I was the runt of the litter. I wasn't! I was just hungry and too weak to fight for food.

Now that we have my real identity cleared up, I can begin to store up in heaven all of my magnificent deeds that I intend to do while on earth.

Thanks for being such a great Heavenly Dog Father and placing me into such a loving home.

Thank you,
Miss Angel Jeannette

(If I hadn't rescued her she would be caught in the revolving rescue door)

Bless This Yummy Food

For: Rev Keith Furrow

Please bless this food to the nourishment of my body. I pray you heal any imperfections in my body. I pray you watch over...Then if I'm not in a rush; I name all the family members, etc and then ask for healing or blessings for what is appropriately needed at the time.

Rev Keith Furrow

P.S. My goal in life: is to be the person my dog thinks I am. We taught Precious Fiona Rose to pray before she eats when she was a small puppy. To this day she will wait to pray before she eats. I pick up her front paws up and put them together. This is base of what we pray. I speak in first person for her.

"My goal in life: is to be the person my dog thinks I am."

Nala My Heart

For: Romano Quattropanetti Beagleandia

Dear Heavenly Dog Father,

For you, the archangel Raffaele and all of the angels surrounding Nala, with your loving and healing, I welcome you to help make me feel in a way that the process of recovery can occur without obstacles, inviting a miracle that you are already here. In your ears. I remember you helped me to have faith and confidence. Nala can experience that now with you.

Thank you! Nala

"Padre dolcissimo,

a te, all'arcangelo Raffaele e agli angeli chiedo di circondare Nala della con la vostra energia amorevole e risanatrice. Vi prego di aiutare Nala a sentirsi in pace, di modo che il processo di guarigione possa avvenire senza ostacoli. Inviateci un miracolo, sapendo che tutto è già sanato ai vostri occhi. Vi chiedo di aiutarmi ad avere fede e fiducia affinchè Nala possa sperimentare subito il vostro amore."

Grazie! Nala

Remi's Prayers for Mommy

For: Raquel Montoya

Dear Heavenly Dog Father,

Heavenly Dog Father, I ask that you please surround my Mommy with your most trusted angel. To watch and protect as she did me. Mommy and I understood each others pain because we both had sick bodies. I heard my Mommy pray a couple of nights to you, I believe. She used to say it will break my heart to lose my girl but I love her so much I don't want her in pain. My Mommy will tell you that I was her Nurse, her best friend and her rock. I didn't want to leave her but she said it would be okay. I left behind a little brother and a little sister. I think they will take care of her the best they can, but I need my Mommy well so that she can love them and take care of them as she took care and loved me. This I ask in your name Heavenly Dog Father.

Love you Forever,
Remi

P.S. I wrote something totally different but as I was texting this to you. It was as if Remi took over my hands and heart.. This is really her word.

My Precious Tina

For: Carmelo Abela

Dear Heavenly Dog Father,

My beloved owner Carmelo is my true inspiration. I am totally relaxed when we are together and, best of all, I feel so safe. The only thing is missing are words. I know he told the almighty Heavenly Dog Father that it was hard for him to say the right words expressing how he feels.

I will be forever grateful to the wonderful Russian lady named Marina Uritskaya who brought me to him. What a lovely gesture she did. Pure kindness!

I have filled his life again to make him whole. We are whole. He told the Heavenly Dog Father that he was really sad when his beloved Titti crossed the rainbow bridge.

Love Tina
(In memory of Titti)
As a black and tan cocker spaniel

Paul And The Sprit Of Gutmeister

For: Paul Warm

Dear Heavenly Dog Father,

Your, So far away
Guts / The Gutmiester
I miss you, everyday.
God, Why?
Did you, Take him away...
I will ask you, again
When, I pray.
Please, grant me a wish
That, I will see him again
One day.
When I take, my final rest.
If you let us, be together

That, would be The Best
With, a broken heart
Please, hear me cry.
I miss The Gutmiester
So much
I can't wait, till I die.
Then, we'll be together
In Heaven, FOREVER...
Peace

—Paul Warm

I know this was supposed to be from Gutmeister but he died before he could write it, so I wrote it. So I did in order to heal and honor his spirit.

Give Momma Comfort
For: Penelope Pews

Dear Heavenly Dog Father,

Now I lay me down to snore. I give my soul to you My Lord. If I should pass before I wake. Give Momma comfort, when me you take. Please Dear Heavenly Dog Father help Momma win her battle against the many diseases she suffers from. Help her find ways to provide for our family without her having to work so hard. Please help her not worry so much about everything. Please give us many years together, for I know she will be heartbroken when I pass for Momma loves me so much and we love Momma so much too. And always help Momma stay strong in her faith in you, Dear Lord. Amen. Also help her remember to give me lots of treats and give me more than my sister.

Thanks Heavenly Dog Father!
That's Bella Boo's aka Penelope Pews Prayer.

"If I should pass before I wake. Give Momma comfort, when me you take."

Buddy's Prayers Of Healing

For: Jim Dovel, Veteran

Dear Heavenly Dog Father,

I want to ask forgiveness for making my Dad upset. He really didn't know how sick I was. He took me to the Vet. And the Vet told him that I would be OK for a couple weeks. I had no way of telling my Dad that I had a tumor in my stomach. The Vet was wrong; I had this tumor for a long time. Not all humans have the answers. I could see my Dad was upset from heaven, so you sent my friend to help. Humans are so fragile. My friend, whose name was the same as mine, kept my Dad company for over two hours. Since I've been here in heaven I have got to meet with my older sister Babe, and she introduced me a few of her older sisters. It might be fun here in Heaven. Babe seems to be the fun one, but Honey, and Punkin are a little standoffish. Oh well, please tell my Dad "I Love Him." And I hope to see him again here in Heaven. Amen.

Yours,
Buddy

Mummies Baby

For: Lee (Rand)

Dear Heavenly Dog Father,

I was a tiny 6 week old pup, also the runt of the litter.

One day this lady came to visit me and my bro's and sis. I had no idea who she was but she lifted me up and gave me a cuddle... then that was it....

After another 2 weeks I was leaving my 1st family to start a new life, and oh boy was I excited.

Over the years, I've had the best walkies and cuddles and got away with a lot of things I shouldn't have done

When I was 3 years old, I saved mum and my bro from carbon monoxide poisoning as I kept barking at mum to wake up. Eventually she did and was saved. I'm her little hero. My mum always says I'm her baby and little angel and savior but realistically mummy saved me.

Lovingly,
Boomer

My Best Friends Doggies Prayer

For: Nicole Richardson

Dear Heavenly Dog Father,

I pray that my best friends will go to heaven

Because I believe all dogs will.

I pray that my dogs can have what ever they want and that's to eat their favorite meal

I pray that my best friends can greet me at the gate

To only put a big smile on my face

I pray that my best friends can take long walks with me and be able to run play by the ocean side

Hop in the car with the air blowing in their hair in the ride

I love my best friends and this prayer is for the fury loves

I pray this best friend's doggie prayer.

Love,
Sabastian & Nyla

A Full Heart

For: Angie Pizelo

Dear Heavenly Dog Father,

Angie and Nicole, my best friends, we are all are a life form of source energy all pieced together as one, in this thing we call physical life.

And I know that my love for all is revealed tenfold in what I do and what I am. I know that I am a loving presence for Angie and a safe place.

Angie fulfills my every need such as food water and shelter. Every night we love to look out of the window with all the lights on to see the gorgeous animals, like the deer and raccoons. I feel so blessed with this life Angie and Nicole have granted me. It is such an honor to be beside them.

Love,
G.G.

"I feel so blessed with this life."

I Miss You So Terribly

For: Lynn Bonham, President Russell Rescue

Dear Heavenly Dog Father,

I will forever be grateful that you brought Mommy into my life. I was homeless and neglected. I was horribly over-bred. You brought her in the shelter and back in isolation to meet me. She reached right down and picked up all five and half pounds, not even noticing that everyone else was afraid of me. I had tried to bite them all. She hugged me and said your name will be Gracie. She told me I was a toy fox terrier.

She was going to foster me for New Rattitudes Washington State. Well Lord, I never left. She loved me so much! We went everywhere together!

I am home now with you Lord. But I watch over my Mommy from the rainbow bridge everyday. Thank you Lord for taking care of my Mommy!

She has Pixie now but still thinks about me everyday. Please open her heart again so she can bond with people. Pixie has been there eight months now and my Mommy still misses me too much. Please tell her it's ok.

Love,
Gracie

"Izzy"

For: Mark Brown

Dear Heavenly Dog Father,

They found me carelessly thrown away
With my mom and sister on that day
We made it a brand new state
And from there it must be fate
You came to meet me
I was so full of love
You hugged and kissed me
A love from above
Your patience and your gentle touch
Made me realize I love you so much
It brings me such joy to show I care
From that lick on you face
To my loving state
I please you and tease you with my favorite ball
I will love you forever
Winter, summer, spring and fall
Our time together is much too short
But of this, I am sure
I could not have found a daddy
Whose love is so pure....

Love,
Izzy

My Life

For: Mikayla Feehan

Dear Heavenly Dog Father,

Sis, woof . . . Have we had a lifetime of memories or what? Over the past 15 years, I have watched you grow from a small child into an adult. I know I won't always be here, but I just want to tell you that I am so proud of the person you have become, while I still am. And even when I'm not around anymore, I don't want you to forget that. Thank you for playing with me, taking me outside, and loving me unconditionally, along with the rest of the family. We have lost a few good ones along the way over the years, but we have all remained so strong together. I pray that you live a fulfilled life, with lots of smiles and love, and I promise to guide you every step of the way.

With the greatest love, and sloppiest of kisses,
Cooper Feehan

My "Bestest" Human

For: Michael Neuner

Dear Heavenly Dog Father,

You are my Special Human. Thank you for another day with you. I see you coming and going and you never forget me. I look forward to seeing you everyday in your busy life. The running, playing, yummy treats and all the kisses. Even the shortest of times are truly amazing. I now look forward to my cuddling up to you for our sleep time. Until tomorrow with my best human.

Love,
My Dog

"Thank you for another day with you."

Family Prayers

For: Taylor Mock

Dear Heavenly Dog Father,

Thank you for giving me my two best friends whom I proudly call mom and dad

Help them forgive me when I bark at scary dogs - my past is not my fault

Give me strength to keep them safe during lightning and fireworks

Grant me courage to protect the house while they are gone

May they never tire and always have energy to play

And always be in good health for walks

Thank you for giving them patience

I pray love for my parents

We pray love for our dog

Thank you for his ceaseless affection

May he never grow old and lose ability to walk

Give him a jovial spirit and energy to play with his toys

Shower him with courage and protection when home alone

Give him peace and calm his anxiety during fireworks and lightning

Help him forgive when we anger at his reactions - his past is not his fault

Thank you for giving us our best friend and the gift of being his mom and dad.

With Love,
Dash

Toys, Toys and More Toys

For: Alexander Dumonde

Dear Heavenly Dog Father,

I just don't understand why you didn't create me just like my brother Odinn who drops a ball immediately after fetching it. Instead, you instilled in me the belief that fetching is way beneath me.

So instead I refuse to let go of the toys! Heavenly Dog Father I know that this tug of war has gone on for a while. Give me that, give it, give it!

Ok I win, I always win. Maybe this is why I never let it go, to prove a point.

Lovingly,
Frigga

"... I refuse to let go of the toys!"

The Other Side

For: Lisa Grajek

Dear Heavenly Dog Father,

I don't feel well. I have been to the vet and they have done many things to me I don't understand. My human says everyone is trying to help me, but I can see it in their eyes. They are worried and afraid and don't have any answers. I feel that my time is coming to an end. I see it in my human's eyes as he holds me and cries. I have served my human for only two short years. Day and night I watch over him. I have stood strong by his side. I have served him with undying loyalty and love. But now, I feel I can serve him no more. Please God, find my human another dog that can replace the love I have for him. One that would lay down his life for his safety. One that will bring joy to his heart and a smile to his face. One who will comfort him when he is afraid and when he thinks of the days we had together.

Love,
Spirit

Athena's Prayers For Her Family

For: Rev John Karn

Dear Heavenly Dog Father,

Please take care of my daughter, Thea when I'm no longer able or no longer here. Please bless my dads and give them all they need to have a happy secure life. Teach Zeplin to know that he is safe and secure. I pray that he eats all his food every day so that his dad will be happy. Please teach the little baby boy to be a mature responsible man. Most of all love both of my dads as much as they have shown that love to me.

AAAAA men.
Athena

"Please bless my dads and give them all they need to have a happy secure life."

Pooh's Prayers

For: Pam Butman

Dear Heavenly Dog Father,

Jeez, my heart just skipped a beat thinking of this…
My Pooh's prayer would be "Mommy and Daddy, may
The Heavenly Dog Father watch over you to be safe
& healthy so you can come home to me and we can be
together for a long, long, long time."

Thank you,
Pooh

Gunner's Love

For: Ken Fraser

Dear Heavenly Dog Father,

Please help my human, Ken. He suffers from chronic morning headaches. As he sits on the couch with ice packs on his head, I climb up in his lap and do my best to help him by snuggling up and letting him know that I am here for him. Thank You for healing his body so we can enjoy this life together.

Your faithful servant Dachshund,
Gunner

"Thank You for healing his body so we can enjoy this life together."

Marley Makes A Difference

For: Scott Mc Michael

Dear Heavenly Dog Father,

I want my daddy Scott to move smoothly out of his bad marriage. He can barely buy groceries and keep the roof over our heads.

Once Scott got married, his wife quit her job and spent every penny he had on a new car, clothes and jewelry. Worst of all I worry about my daddy going bankrupt. And where are we going to live if he does?

Signed,
Marley

My Lynn

For: Lynn Cullens

Dear Heavenly Dog Father,

Please help my beloved owner get rid of her stomach cancer. She shows me a brave face, but I know differently. How does a dog cope with this? Am I supposed to be strong and bold like a lion? But what if I don't feel like it? I am crushed as I watch her whittle away. I ask You, Heavenly Dog Father, what you would do if you were in my same "Paws?"

Love,
Ophelia

"Please help my beloved owner get rid of her stomach cancer."

I Love You So Much

For: Simon Alpert

Dear Heavenly Dog Father,

Simon, I love u more than anything. U treat me w soo much love 'n' attention even got my cataract removed. U had great patience w the healing process. U didn't care about the costs. U took excellent care of me. Thank u from the bottom of my heart.

Amen
Abraham

Daddy Don't Leave!

For: Matt DeMeyer

Dear Heavenly Dog Father,

Jenny says to me daily with her sweet face and eyes, "Dad, don't leave me at home, I want to go to work. I want to see all the clients! I pray you take me with you every day!"

Lovingly,
Jenny

"Dad, don't leave me at home."

G.G. Knows Best!

For: Angie and Stella Pizelo

Dear Heavenly Dog Father,

I pray that my "grand dog" mom and my "grand dog" dad are safe from harm's way. As you know there are plenty of wild critters with huge teeth that roam the Sierras.

Heavenly Dog Father, you deliberately placed me with Angie and Stella to keep them safe. With a little help from above I know I can.

Love And Kisses,
G.G.

My Patty Loves Me

For: Quinn Alexander Fontaine

Dear Heavenly Dog Father,

"Quinn, I'm so beyond proud of the beautiful, integrated and gentle MAN you've become. I joined your family when you were just four years old. I could already feel your pain at being a boy trapped in a girl's body. I knew before you did and it only made me love you more! I took great pride in holding space for you and your tenderness back then and even now. I've always been with you and love that we both get to celebrate your life now that you have transitioned. I see you doing wonderful things in service to humanity and the paradigm of love. In all you do, please remember to always love yourself and honor your path. You have come so far, sweet boy! Know too that you can always call on me and I'll be there either in your lap or kissing your face. Thank you for teaching me so much about acceptance, embodiment, hope and love! Now go play and pay it all forward!"

Love and Kisses,
Patty

P.S. Patty died when I was 18

Prayers From The Paws

For: Scott McMichael

Dear Heavenly Dog Father,

Thank you for my earthly home, I know you hand-picked my family to love and care for. They treat me well and I will continue to follow your example of agape love. They don't really know you sent me, but hopefully with time they will grow to understand. I have one request, that when I come home you will send a replacement quickly; I am not sure how they would manage without the presence of Godly love you provide through us.

Signed,
Your Faithful Servant,
Hopeful

Shanies Mom

For: Docteures Giselle

Dear Heavenly Dog Father,

"The Mommy needs your help." You see, she had been trying
to find me as I was reaching out to her because I didn't feel well.
She always made me feel better. I just wanted her touch. But...I
returned to you before she could help me, which has caused her to
cry many tears. I know you remember back when I was 6 weeks
old. "The Mommy and "The Boy" came. I was so sick that night
and they told "The Mommy" I was not a good dog and she needed
to return me and get her money back because I might not live to be
a year old. They also told her that I would not walk correctly but
"The Mommy," through your guidance and her healing, made me
well and made sure I walked; I ran and could even dance whenever
she wanted. She massaged my hips everyday and made sure I was
always with her, the boy, the man and the baby. Right now Heavenly
God Father let "The Mommy" know that I am free; my weakened
physical body does not bind me anymore. I was willing to go
because you promised me she would eventually find out where I was
and what happened to me. This was the only way that I could protect
her life, and I did. Please ease her pain now by letting her finally
know that she could not have saved me because the "Toxic Mold
Poisoning" had caused my organs to fail. She learned that she had
been poisoned just like me but there was time to save her life. You
see, "The Mommy" had no idea until then that she was dying too.
She's alive and has so much more to do. I visit her often. I keep her
company when she is alone. I know she loved me as I loved her, the
boy, the man and the baby. "The Boy" and his babies are apart of my
pack, too. Being here with You, Heavenly God Father, I get to watch
over everybody.

After all we helped each other...because she lived, I lived and
my leaving helped her to live on.

Love, SHANE

My Loving Family

For: Margaret Moritz, Coley, Terry, and Aunt Catherinel

Dear Heavenly Dog Father,

My name is Pandora. I live in Carlsbad. I am a Rhodesian Ridgeback and Pitbull (it makes me sad that pitbulls have such a bad rap when I love people so much). I live with Coley,(my owner and best friend) and with Coley's Mom and daddy, Terry.

I have the best life. Coley just turned 30 and I just turned 13. Now I'm older and not doing so well now , but I'm so cheerful that I have the best life. Everyone is so good to me. Coley sleeps downstairs on the couch these days so I can sleep close to her on my dog bed, because I cannot make it up the stairs anymore to my room.

Coley was studying to take the MCATS test and changed her goal to homeopathic medicine. I pray for her success and am so proud of her. She is just brilliant and has an amazing memory and dedicates herself to learning everything she can to help others to be well, especially me. She has me on a healthy lean meat-and-vegetable diet, gives me turmeric and Move Free Ultra to extend my quality of life.

I pray for her Mom and Daddy Terry that they keep the faith and stay, calm, sweet, and supportive of Coley. Coley always makes me laugh... because sometimes she talks for me and uses a Spanish accent. I originally lived with a Spanish family when I was a little puppy, but I've been working every day to perfect my English.

I pray that Coley knows she will always be in my heart. I pray that she knows how lucky she is to have me and how lucky I am to have her. I pray that Coley stays as happy as possible and that she does this world with absolute confidence. She's the smartest, logical person I know, and I should know cause I've hung out with some pretty crazy people.

I also pray that her mother continues to notice me through the patio door and gives me a doggie treat when I give her my sweetest stare. The main thing is I say is "Thank You, God, for my family, that always loves me and always takes care of me—Coley, Mom, Terry, and aunt Catherine."

Love, Pandora

Isn't God Amazing?

For: Morgan Hartt

Dear Heavenly Dog Father,

God is great!
As I recognize that I am one with the Eternal God,
And that I am perfect and whole as God created me,
As I recognize and acknowledge this fact, I also
acknowledge it for my master.
I am of God, You are of God; we are of God.
May you be blessed.
I give thanks to God in all things for myself and my
master.

Lovingly,
Emma Louise

"I give thanks to God in all things for myself and my master."

My Lovely Lillie

For: Alicia Harmon

Dear Heavenly Dog Father,

I pray for my Mommy Alicia to be happy and to not be so stressed. I can see it in her eyes.

Love, Lillie

Ps. Miss Lillie is an empathic and feels when I am down or stressed out.

She is 13 now and we are very connected. She is definitely an old soul and has since passed since I wrote this.

My Lola

For: Charles Dougherty

Dear Heavenly Dog Father,

I pray "Please come back from work early!! I miss you while you are away."

Love,
Lola

"I miss you while you are away."

Angels Gather Around

For: Leisa Grajek

Dear Heavenly Dog Father,

Angels go to my Nikko's new home. Find him and comfort him; any new transition is hard. I picture him happy and secure.

My dog is feeling low, an infection is being treated. Please make the medication heal his wound.

It's a religious experience to listen to a young Rooster start to crow. How he struggles with his new voice.

Love Your Servant,
Jenny

There Is Freedom In The Clouds

For: Laura Mullins

Dear Heavenly Dog Father,

When you're walking down the streets with me on your mind, I'm walking in your footsteps only half a step behind and when it's time for you to go home from that body to be free. Remember you're not going; you're coming here to me.

Love,
Angel

"Remember you're not going; you're coming here to me."

Our Masters

For: Morgan And All Dogs

Dear Heavenly Dog Father,

We pray for our masters...
May you find peace in the quiet moments of your
dawn.
Whenever and wherever that may be.
In walks with us along the beach.
Quiet time with us at home.
We ask God to let us create a perfect moment for you.
As we greet you with kisses, when you get home...
Or wake you up with enthusiasm in the morning...
Or bring you to laughter at our antics.
Since they have blessed us dear God, we now ask that
you bless them.

With Love,
Emma Louise
Morgan's Baby

Karma Is A Bitch

For: Angie Lewis

Dear Heavenly Dog Father,

I pray that the Souls of those Individuals who have abused, mistreated and mutilated innocent Creatures shall be returned into the Bodies of the same Creatures they have violated and suffer the same fate.

Lovingly,
Angeldreams

"I pray for all the innocent creatures."

Amazing Grace

For: Sharon Jackson

Dear Heavenly Dog Father,

God's amazing "Grace" is the name given to me,
On my master's and friend's heart God's grace set her free…
Diligently I watch her seeking the word of God to grow inside,
Savoring the power in her heart to hide….
Asking for the Holy Spirit to abide in her heart, mind, and soul
Making Jesus Christ first in her life is her goal…
Away and forever her eyes fix on things above,
Zestfully and cheerfully seeking His undying love…
In her loving arms she takes such good care of me,
Now and forever with her I want to be…
Giving her my protection, friendship, companionship and love,
God, thank You for bringing us together, we praise you above…
Raising me has brought her so much joy.
As she played and trained me with my special toy…
Clearly, she loves me with all her heart.
Easily I have love for her from the start.

With so much gratitude,
God's Amazing Grace

Bella My Love

For: John Mills

Dear Heavenly Dog Father,

I am so grateful that you brought me into such
a loving family. I loved my parents so much while
they were alive. They have since passed as a result of
Alzheimer's. They suffered so much.

Heavenly Dog Father, You have since blessed me with
their son John, whom I love so much. I'm grateful that he
loves me unconditionally - including when I bark at the
neighbor's cat in the middle of the night. I pray he is safe
in this night and brings home a "Bella Bag." Thank God
for leftovers... Amen

We are filled with love and joy even thought it is now
just the two of us. We follow your will, dear Heavenly
Dog Father, on what you desire of us everyday. Thank
You also for our health and our great love for each other.

Love, Bella

Miss Charlotte's Puppy Prayer

For: Hannah Mullins

Dear Heavenly Dog Father,

My mom left me home alone again, so I'm putting my puppy paws together to pray for her.

The thought of my night time ear rubs and morning butt scratches have been getting me through the long and lonely days.

Please help my mom be more in the moment... just like me! Guide her to spend less time working and more time letting me give her kisses and snuggles.

I know my mom cheats on me with other dogs when she goes somewhere called "work," but I forgive her, and I hope you will too. Nothing will stop me from loving her!

I do wish it wasn't so easy for her to leave me every morning. I sit on her to keep her from going, but she just smothers me with mom kisses, hides some treats around the house, and takes off. I know she loves me very much, but I don't know how she goes all day without seeing her little girl!

Do you know what that creepy thing called "Furbo" is? For some reason, I feel like I'm always being watched!

It might not seem like it, but I know my mom needs me. Please let me live a really long time, so I can keep her heart whole.

Love,
Apup

A Prayer To Heal All

For: Tom Schenck

Dear Heavenly Dog Father,

I ask you for divine intervention for my mom and dad. I pray that You, Heavenly Dog Father, instill in them a sense of strength and peace.

Several months ago, my beloved mom Nancy fell down a flight of stairs and almost left us. Then out of the blue, you touched her with your ray of sunshine. Your healing graces allowed her to slowly recover from her traumatic brain injury. It has truly been a rocky path that I can share my knowledge with other dogs what a traumatic brain injury actually means.

Heavenly Dog Father, did you know that Tom and Nancy have been married forty awesome years? And that they are best of friends experiencing every season life has to offer.

Thanks to the intervention of your loving paws and the grace of heaven's healing light Nancy is once again speaking to us in her loving voice.

With loving appreciation,
Boyd

Molly And Bill

For: Bill Kutschman

Dear Heavenly Dog Father,

Molly here. The black lab mix. Aka. Billy's owner. Just thought I would check in. Kinda a progress report if you will, as we both know a while back you assigned me a special adoption case. A hooman known as Billy. I've got to admit I had some doubts at first, worried I'd bitten off more than I could chew. I mean, after all he was pretty far gone downright feral. Very aloof untrusting, almost scared to be loved. But Lord, I know that through you all things are possible, so I didn't give up on him. Make no mistake; he's been a hard nut to crack. I decided to jump in head first. I showed him all the love, patience and devotion I could muster and I'm here to say it paid off. His heart finally melted from within that block of ice that had surrounded it. Lord, I know that all dogs go to heaven, so with that said can you also prepare a place for my hooman, Billy. For as it appears we made it after all.

Love,
Molly

Can You Save Mommy And Daddy?

For: Jordan Gunn

Dear Heavenly Dog Father,

We need your help to stop the kid's dad from drinking until he passes out! I worry he will die early and leave the kids without a dad. I see that he is not the best example.

My momma needs to stop doing things that turn out really bad, which later on she regrets. I get upset too. I can only imagine how she feels.

Please step in with your loving paw and help save our family.

Worrying myself sick,
Zion

"Please step in with your loving paw and help save our family."

Bless All Dogs

For: Clarence Wise

Dear Heavenly Dog Father,

I pray may God bless all of the dogs in the world. I am eleven years old, a Shih Tzu show puppy. I am like a kid, love to have fun and know about peoples needs. I love my master so much.

Love,
Faithful

Suzie's Heartfelt Prayers
For: Bill Emeno

Dear Heavenly Dog Father,

Please help keep my master focused, making it happen with your divine grace. Please bless his new business venture, attracting the right people with the right intentions to work with him.

Heavenly Dog Father, You have a better perspective from above than I. I am way too short to see anything. But you are tall and a mighty Heavenly Dog Father.

I pray you fill my master with peace day by day, giving him love and strength.

Lovingly,
Suzy Q

"I pray you fill my master with peace day by day..."

We Pray For Peace
For: Kevin Monohan

Dear Heavenly Dog Father,

Please fill Kevin with Your spirit and bless him with your peace and grace. May he be slow to anger and quick to forgive.

I pray that You, Heavenly Dog Father, open his heart to accept the love of Val and bless their relationship as they grow together honoring one another. That will make me so skip with joy!

Love,
Molly

P.S. She was a rescue from Mexico. Love her so much!

Dreams

For: Steven Golden

Dear Heavenly Dog Father,

I know that this is supposed to be a prayer from Rozi to me. But she told me to offer a prayer from me to you.

My beautiful Rozi, I remember the day I that I came to get you from the breeder. Your beautiful blue eyes looked into my soul and I knew we were destined to be together. Our time on this planet was brief yet so full of joy and for that I carry with me in my heart always. You were always such a great friend and always happy to see me.

Often I hear her speak to me, telling me that everything is going to be ok.

Love,
"Steven" For Rozi

Standing Tall

For: Melody Matthews

Dear Heavenly Dog Father,

Lord, help us continue to light up, bring healing, and love our sweet Melody. She holds on to the past, and doesn't love herself as we love her. We are concerned for her life, especially when the ambulance came. We know her unconditional moment of love was when we caught her throwing up as we saw Your Great Hand hold her hair back. We know a peace that passes her understanding. Help her find this as we lay with her. Infuse her with your grace. Help her to let go of her mistakes. She is afraid often, and needs to fully know as we do that you love her. Thank You that she chose life. Thank You that she rejects death every day, chooses to love by eating your food. She prays for us everyday, and at the same time, has no idea how much we do for her. Time is short, and she is scared she will not see us again. Help her give her fears to you; receive your and Our forgiveness. Thank You for giving us to her to show her that there is a God that is slow to anger, quick to be compassionate, see her as an instrument, not an ornament as the world does. Help her know that in the infinite light, all things work together for good. She has her earthly father confused with you though he does the best he can. Help her see You as we do. Reveal that you are a God of love, not harsh criticism or anger. Help her understand others as we do. Give her our patience, tenderness, and childlike spirit. Bring back her joy and laughter. We do not allow comparison to steal ours. We know that fear is a liar. Let her know it is. Give her energy to enjoy creation outside again, walk us, and see Your Beauty in the little things in life. Help her to see us, really see us... Not just what we do, but who we are. Help her to see her heart, how big it is, instead of what is in her wallet. Help her see that what matters is how much she truly loves. We are her rays of light, help us shine bright like the Sun. Help her light shine in the darkness, be a beacon in the night, unafraid to call you her God, for you are her guiding light. May your power rest upon her, for Your strength will help her through. Help her know we will never let go. Help her to look to you. Thank You for all the many blessings she gives us. She loves us more than she knows. We thank you for a home, food, love, and the simple things she brings. Bless her as you bless us. Help her to be unselfish as we are. Help her to trust as we do. Help her to rest as we do. In Your love and light, Amen.

Grace Be With You,
Love Her Doggie

My Soul

For: Kathryn Evans

Dear Heavenly Dog Father,

An ode to my guardian

Please do not grieve nor think of me with tears. It was heaven beside you.

I feel you and see you everyday from across the rainbow bridge.

We had so much love, fun and togetherness.

I am your forever dog, an unconditional love that can never be matched.

I look over You and know that Mya, Dewett, and now Mickey are all in my heart, but would never take your place.

I am joyous and free and frolicking in green fields everyday.

We will be reunited someday, and remember please do not hurry the process, as it is a true blessing to be on Earth.

And having you as my guardian and best friend was my greatest blessing.

The light is always shining on me and the wind blowing through my hair.

I protect you in heaven as I did on Earth.

Love and light and wet sloppy kisses,

Your best friend always,

Love, Boomer

P.S. I cried a lot writing it. I LOVED my boy SO MUCH!!! I love all of my dogs, but he was my first pet and stole my heart, for sure! I am so happy that you are going to have him in your book. In honor of him and the legacy he left with me and those who knew him. :) I can't wait to buy the book.

The Journey
For: Steve Knight

Dear Heavenly Dog Father,

Hope your day is as good as my day! We are looking forward to barking at you upon your return and giving you lots of kisses and tail wags. May you see the beauty in more than you imagined.

Love Lola And Oliver

"We are looking forward to barking at you upon your return..."

Penny's Wishes

For: Jimmy Hilgados

Dear Heavenly Dog Father,

I know that you are not well and soon to have an operation. My prayer for you is to store up your treasures up in heaven like you always tell others. I see you being so kind to strangers every day, giving them the clothes off your back and money to buy food. You have such a big heart and you have taught me so much to be kind to other dogs.

Heavenly Dog Father, You always said life here is very temporary and we are judged by our acts here on earth.

Lovingly,
Britches

Oh My Heart

For: Michael Zentner

Dear Heavenly Dog Father,

I have a bunch of prayers that I say every day for my master.

Please make him full before he finishes that plate of food so I get the rest.

Please bring him home safe tonight so we can snuggle some more and enjoy snacks together!

And lastly, please don't let him know I'm the one who buried his hat in the yard! I only did it because I missed him, but he gets so angry!

Love,
Bebe

"Please make him full before he finishes that plate of food so I get the rest."

I Am Filled With Love For You

For: Diane Mc Michael

Dear Heavenly Dog Father,

Some days my owner comes home and you can tell she's defeated. On these days, I do my best to be extra good. I don't spill any water or track any dirt inside from our daily walks. When we sit down, I lay my head on her lap. I sometimes feel helpless. I love seeing her smile, and when she is in this mood it makes me sad. Maybe you can gift me with knowing how to do a new trick so I can make her excited. After she rescued me, all I want to do is rescue her back.

Love,
All Dogs

"After she rescued me, all I want to do is rescue her back."

Peggy Sue Means You

For: Kevin Kantner

Dear Heavenly Dog Father,

Hi!! It's Peggy Sue Kantner and my prayer today is for Kevin my owner. Sure seems like he's been under a lot of stress lately worrying about his health and finances. Please take a minute to look down on him and help us through this rough time. If it's not too much trouble... Please remind him that I really like treats!

Thanks!!!
Love,
Peggy Sue

Our Blessed Guardian

For: George Noujaim

Dear Heavenly Dog Father,

Find homes for the ones waiting to be adopted, especially the ones that were displaced from the fires and went back only to find no one was there. Please hold on Sparky. Someone is interested in adopting you.

Love,
Sparky And All Rescues

"Find homes for the ones waiting to be adopted."

My Doggie Rascal

For: Landon Kroger (9 years old)

Dear Heavenly Dog Father,

I want to tell you why I love Rascal so much. I know this is supposed to be from Rascal but I wanted you to hear from me just how special he is in my life. Please give him a gold collar.

My dog Rascal is the cutest dog ever,
He is lazy and funny and also very clever.
When he was younger he escaped over the wall and climbed up tree,
That is over 10 feet tall.

Rascal likes to sleep on the floor by my bed,
And I can reach down and scratch him on the head.
He rolls on his back and kicks his feet in the air,
He does crazy things without a care.
I love my doggie and I take him on walks.
We go down the street and around the block.
My dog Rascal means a lot to me,
And is my doggie and will always be.

Love,
Rascal's best friend Landon

Embracing The Light

For: Tania Fairchild

Dear Heavenly Dog Father,

Thank You for blessing me with my forever family. They gave me the best life any dog could ask for. I had a little girl to watch over and cats to herd. My dog sister and dog brother were treasured companions. I even had a great Papa.

I spent lot of time with him. I am thankful that I was there to comfort my family when Papa went to heaven. And now that I have crossed the rainbow bridge I hope to bring comfort to my family. I have been reunited in heaven with my siblings that passed before me, but more importantly I am reunited with my Papa eating snacks and watching Westerns.

Love, Murphy
(In memory of Jim)

The "Look"

Alexander Dumonde

Dear Heavenly Dog Father,

You must have had a paw in naming me Frigga Agape because you saw that I embodied all that is good about love.

When I came into my parents lives, I was a tiny thing with a large head, and now they tell me I am beautiful, well-mannered Jack Russell that just wants to lick my mom and dad and show them that I love them.

Heavenly Dog Father, You have allowed me to rule the universe with my looks.

I wonder why on earth my dad isn't fetching me a towel since I just came out of the lake 'eh?

Silent treatment?

My humble servant dad begs your forgiveness and he will be back with that towel swiftly for the queen.

Queen,
Frigga Agape

We Love All Dogs!

For: Steve Ronce

Dear Heavenly Dog Father,

Oh Heavenly Dog Father, Giver of All Life, thank You for giving us dogs, Lord! The love of a dog is immeasurable. I pray all dogs find a Home to be loved in, Lord. Dogs have brought so much joy to us God. We pray Lord that You Bless us with the confidence to accept and share this Love! We pray Heavenly Dog Father. Amen.

Love and Kisses,
Stella

Abby And Mack

For: Jim Gibbons

Dear Heavenly Dog Father,

Abby and Mack up in heaven, we miss you every day and still hear your paws in the hall clicking at night. You are never forgotten, sweet angels, and Fiona, Fergus and Bella are all here celebrating your memories every day. We miss you and love you so much!

Love,
Fiona, Fergus and Bella

From My Heart…We have an old girl Fiona who has been with my wife for 1/3 of her life. She will be 18 in June. Has had Addison's for 10 years. Blind and deaf and has dementia but we love her so much. This may be her last year, and sometimes we wonder if we are selfishly keeping her alive, but she is still our baby Fizzy Bear and we sing to her, "Fizzy Bear Fizzy Bear you have no underwear and go everywhere, Fizzy Bear our sweet Fizzy Bear." She wanders around the back yard still and she is our angel on earth. We dread the inevitable as it will put me in the hospital like when her sister Abby passed in 2015 from kidney failure induced by Addison's. I am a big strong guy built like an Ex NFL lineman yet these dogs are so much more than just dogs it just gets me to my core. Excuse the tautology.

My Adoptive Parents

For: Maria Diaz

Dear Heavenly Dog Father,

I pray for my adoptive parents as they begin their life together, I hope that everyday is filled with love, respect for each other, and please don't let them forget about their baby dog "Pinky."

I pray that they are always healthy so we can continue to enjoy those wonderful walks around the block, and pray they always have a job so they can buy my dog toys and dog food, I pray that they always love me and take care of me the way they do.

Love,
Pinky

My Angel

For: Evelyn Peterson

Dear Heavenly Dog Father,

Hoping you are giving a lot of loving care to my sweet Angel. She was always very special and tried to please without making a fuss. I've never had a dog like her; she was very mellow and did silly things, like getting behind curtains with her head peeking out. She didn't bark much, only to tell we had company at the door, but was very friendly to everyone she met. Angel didn't lick you like other dogs; she wanted to smell your hair or ears. There were other special things about her, which only make me wish I could have protected her from getting cancer. After her passing I found a necklace that says how I feel about her.

"If love could have saved you, you would have lived forever!"

Love You Always,
Evelyn and Angel

Heart Of Gold

For: Laura Mullins

Dear Heavenly Dog Father,

These are my prayers...
Treat me kindly my beloved master, for no heart in the world is more grateful for kindness than my loving heart. Don't break my spirit with a stick. Your patience and understanding will quickly teach me more of the things you want me to do. Speak to me often for your voice is the world's sweetest music. When I'm cold and wet bring me inside...now I am a domesticated animal and your devoted worshipper. And, my master, should you see the one deprives me of health and sight, don't turn me away from you. Rather hold me gently because my fate was safest in your hands.

Love,
Angel

My Missy

For: David Irvin For: David Irvin

Dear Heavenly Dog Father,

This is Jasmine. I am worried about my pa and my sister Missy. Missy woke us up real early today. Pa is so worried and sad right now. He says he thinks Missy is dying. I'm not for sure what that means, God, but my pa is really upset. I have never seen him crying before. He is holding Missy and said for me to come over and see her. I think she is really sick or something. Pa just called momma at work and told her that Missy is dying. He is really crying now God! Would you help him and Missy to be better? I'm kind of scared too. Now he says that Missy has died. She's not moving or breathing or anything! Could you please help our family to not be sad? We always thank you for being good to us. Help us to always be good to you, too. Thank you, Heavenly Dog Father. Amen. I am pa to all of our "furries."

From,
Jasmine

My Special Mom

For: Camilla Bullman

Dear Heavenly Dog Father,

Jameson and I want Mommy to be able to work from home making a really good income! We want Mommy to spend more time at home with us.

Love,
Penny & Jameson

"We want Mommy to spend more time at home with us."

Those Impossibly Huge Whales

For: Chuck von Yamashita

Dear Heavenly Dog Father,

Please don't let the whales swallow us or smash us to smithereens. Please guide the swans to their winter home. Let the trails be fast and smooth this winter!

Love,
Paris

Saving Precious Lives

For: Kelly Chaffee

Dear Heavenly Dog Father,

I pray to you tonight as I always do, yet there is a particular subject I am hoping you can help me with. You see my mom has always been in animal rescue and when any animal needed help, she was there doing whatever it took to save that animal. Lately she has been unable to do her rescue work and it troubles her tremendously.

I'm sure you know this but when she began her work at the SPCA years ago, over 28 million dogs and cats were killed each year in animal shelters across the nation. It was 1984 when my mom said "killing dogs and cats is wrong" and she began a mission at her own shelter to stop the killing. That included farm animals that were rescued from cruelty cases as well as dogs and cats. Her boss at the time did not agree with my mom, and each day she was away from work he would have all the dogs in the shelter killed. My mom would come in the next day devastated because she had not been able to get the dogs out. Yet she persevered and eventually the Board of Directors agreed with her that the killing was wrong. Eventually they fired her boss and put her in charge and the killing stopped. Yet that was not normal in a community that was used to killing animals as a means to population control. The community and the media were not kind to her but she refused to kill the dogs and cats in her care and eventually found other communities that felt the same. Together they created a no-kill coalition.

For the next 30 years, the animal shelter was able to save over 40,000 animals. I am one of the beneficiaries of the shelter's work. I came from a puppy mill in Pennsylvania. The shelter that took me from the puppy mill decided to kill my brother and me. We were very frightened of everyone and as Chihuahua mixes, we felt the best way to protect ourselves and each other was to bark loud at and possibly bite those that may look like a threat. Luckily at six months of age, the PA shelter asked the SPCA where my mom volunteered, to take us. Even at the new shelter, we were scared and sometimes tried to bite people. Eventually my mom decided it was time to leave the shelter and knew she should take us home since no one else dared to adopt us. She felt confident the shelter would continue the mission of no-kill. My mom had done her part and was relieved she could finally move on.

But you see Heavenly Dog Father, there is no "moving on" for someone like my mom, someone who cares so deeply for all the dogs, cats, horses, cows, pigs, sheep, goats, etc. There is no moving on when animals are still being killed for food and in the shelters. According to the ASPCA 1.5 million dogs and cats are still being killed in animal shelters each year and 10 BILLION farm animals are killed each year just for food consumption.

My mom is not as active as she once was due to health issues, so she is home with us daily. Sometimes she is so sad about the deaths of all the animals, that she wraps her arms around me and cries softly into my fur. I don't know how to help her without barking and biting those that make her sad, and she tell's me that is not a good thing to do. So I ask You, Dear Heavenly Father, can you please do something to stop or lessen the killing of innocent animals? Is there a way you can shed more kindness into our world? Please, Dear Heavenly Father, show those that are killing animals the way to other means so that the killing will stop. Thank you for listening as I pray to decrease my mom's sad moments.

P.S. Can I ask one more favor? The next time my mom has a family wedding can you PLEASE not allow it to be in Texas? I didn't want my mom to leave me at home and she insisted that my brother and I go, but man was that plane ride was awful!!!

Sincerely,
Mercedes aka "Tadies"

The Holiday King

For: Alexander Dumonde

Dear Heavenly Dog Father,

I know that I am so lucky to go on holidays designed around me! We have to find the most remote cabin in the Northwood's of Wisconsin with a private lake for me to swim and a mile long driveway lined with bushes for me to sniff.

What do I do? Of course I decide to scare off all the beautiful wildlife!

That said, I barked at the black bear eating those blackberries up front scaring him away. I don't think he will be back so long as I am around.

Signed the fierce protector,
Odinn

Those Pearly Gates

For: John Humphrey

Dear Heavenly Dog Father,

When I am about to enter the pearly gates of dog heaven, please don't let any dogs know my age in human years. I would be 1,000 years old!

Love and Kisses,
Darth

"...please don't let any dogs know my age in human years."

Pandora's Gratitude Box

For: Nicole Worley Juliet

Dear Heavenly Dog Father,

HI! My name is Pandora! I'm a pit-bull Rhodesian ridgeback, the best guard dog and sheriff my house will ever know! I've been doing my best dog job at being the best dog for 13 years now, but because I'm older I have to mellow out on keeping the peace. That means I don't bark at those annoying things called "helicopters" or "kites" or "balloons" anymore, and I can't catch squirrels or birds like I used to... But! That's okay, cause my master, Momma, she's taking very good care of me. She knows I don't like being alone, so she sleeps with me, even if that means she has to sleep on the couch cause I can't go upstairs anymore. She knows that I eat too much and too fast, so she makes me small foods many times a day so I don't hurt my tummy. She has been with me since I was two months old and carried me everywhere until I was too heavy. She's really good at being dog mom.

Oh! And Mommas parents are here too, there's blonde mom and dad guy. They are really nice! I like my hoomans! Blonde mom gives me snacks when momma's not home and it makes me really happy! We've got a really good house here! I like that everyone is really nice to me! That's why I'll protect them for as long as I can, no matter what!

But, Heavenly Dog Father, I'm confused and I was hoping you could help me. My master looks sad lately, like when I fall, or when my tummy hurts, or when I trip on stuff. She looks so worried and I don't know why. I know

I'm older now, but I'm still really happy! And I want her to be happy too! I don't really know how this works; asking You for stuff, but do You think You could help her out?

So, I guess since I won't always be around, my dog prayer is, will You look out for my hoomans? You know, make sure that they are always happy and healthy and smiling? Especially my Momma, she's given me the best dog life, so I want her life to be the best too please!

Thank you, love Pandora

Oh!
P.S. Can you please have blonde mom gimme more snacks? Thank you! Amen!

"Can you please have blonde mom gimme more snacks?"

A Treasure

For: Joann Oracx

Dear Heavenly Dog Father,

(Zina's condensed version of her life with me goes something like this)

I am now blind and I have to leave my Joann, who has loved me unconditionally from the time that she bred me with Brutus and Prep Rica. I know that she wanted me to be her breeding female for The Rare Breed of American Bulldogs.

I could not let human beings continue to hurt her and beat her and break her jaws and her bones, so I snapped and I became very protective. The days that I could run without a leash and be free are gone. Remember, I used let the children ride on my back like I was a horse? And say to them to be friendly with all dogs.

I saw my Joanne looking for me. I had to protect her from all harm and I would knock her down, sit on her chest, and growl and snarl. People wanted to take advantage of her because she was so naive and so gracious and giving help to "needy" as a nurse. The world is not like that anymore.

Heavenly Dog Father, I know you are taking my soul away from my Joann, and I can only pray that I can continue to watch out for her. And there will be good Doggies by her side to continue watching out for my Joann the way she has watched out for human kind in the war from 9/11 2001. When all things changed for humanity…..

Forever,
Zina

PS: My mom Joann was a 911 volunteer team rescue nurse to ground Zero on 9/11 2001. She was also a hospice nurse and had to have a tag to get into ground Zero. Can you believe it was harder for Joann to get out of ground Zero then it was for her to get in there? Later on they wanted mom to go work transporting organs for delivery for transplant. Bless her tender heart.

A Prayer From Angus

Written with love by Jacquie and Meghen

Dear Heavenly Dog Father,

I have served my family through the years,
Together we've laughed and shed many tears.
Still I know that I have much to do. My time on earth just can't be through
So I pray to you now
And it comes from the heart
Because one dog must finish what one dog starts
But if I must go
Let it not be this way
Let the time come on some far off day.
I am not asking for world peace
And I am not asking for the moon
But please don't make me leave for this is much too soon.

In Gratitude,
Angus

In Remembrance

For: Diane Highman

Dear Heavenly Dog Father,

"Until one has loved an animal, part of their soul remains unawakened."
My "Golden" Treasure "Hudson" …..I love you more the words can say…

You have brought so much joy and sunshine to my days…
For 12 ½ years you were faithfully by my side helping me through life….
And I wouldn't have missed a single minute of it for the world
Oh…You had so many charms…that brought me laughter, love and sometime tears..

Like when you'd find something on one of our walks (it could be a simple piece of paper)
And you acted like it was the "greatest" treasure! Your eyes would light up and your tail would wag…
And you wanted me to make a big fuss every time….I really think you did it just to make me smile…

I loved the beautiful long locks of hair on your ears and the cute little ridge down your nose…
I remember when your brother Chevy was called to heaven early and I was so heartbroken..
But you looked at me with your beautiful loving golden eyes (that always said so much)
And said Mom…"We" can make it through this…I'm here for you…
Or if I was having a bad day in the office, you'd come say, "Mom let's go for a walk I promise we'll have fun!"

Some of your favorite things (and mine)

"The Shop" Where even on the coldest morning… and it was hard to even walk..
Going with Papa to the shop for a snack was so important to you…he loved you so much…
And then you'd come back and tell me about "ALL" the petting's and

"Love" from the boys in the shop

"The Pond" …I swear our pond was full of magic!
First it starts with the "Gator" ride where you and Bentley would stand so tall and proud in anticipation…
Even on your hardest days, the weight of the world was gone if you were at the pond!
We'd play ball, swim and even catch a goose! And we would just lay in the grass and look up at the sky and talk…

"The Park" also had magic too! You would just come alive! And you'd be off to find your next treasure!
And you loved seeing all your park's buddies…especially "Goob;" you and her would walk at your own pace down the trails..
And you always took control of which way "everyone" would walk… Your way!

I can only hope you enjoyed our life together as much as I…Your brother Bentley and I are lost without you…
But one day will come, when we'll start to see through the pain of the moment, and remember just "you…"
Now you go and play, and look down when you can, remembering we love you, and this isn't the end.

Tuesday 10.29.19
My amazing "best" friend Hudson closed his tired eyes for the last time…a pain that's almost unbearable….
He said Mom…I'm so very tired…please be there with me and help me go to heaven…
With tears in my eyes… and part of my heart…I let you go….

I Love and miss you so much buddie Hudson….You completed my life….
You will always be by my side…and 1 will chat with you in the mornings…..
And "We" will walk together…forever….

In Divine Gratitude

For: Laura Welch

Dear Heavenly Dog Father,

    I want to thank you for my beautiful mom; I love her with all my heart. I know dog is God backwards. That's because dogs are your angels in heaven, dear Heavenly Dog Father. And they are our little Angel's on this earth. Amen.

    I love you Heavenly Dog Father,
Cloie Marie

"...dog is God backwards."

Sasha

For: Nova Gunn

Dear Heavenly Dog Father,

I worry myself to death about the kids' living situation.

Heavenly Dog Father, did you happen to notice there are five mattresses lying on the bedroom floor? There are nine people living in a dinky, two-bedroom apartment.

It is as if we live in poverty. Heavenly Dog Father, do we? You know best.

Please step in to help the family. I worry about the kids riding bikes outside. I have counted a total of six gangs circling around like vultures. What are they after do you know?

Please.

We need your help right now so I can sleep at night!

Kisses,
Sasha

Watch Over Me

For: James Walton

Dear Heavenly Dog Father,

I thank you and your angels for watching over me and allowing me to see another day. You blessings are not taken for granted and I pray you will continue to watch over him. We pray in your name. Amen.

Love,
Fido

"I thank you and your angels for watching over me."

Looking To the Heavens

For: Alexander Dumonde

Dear Heavenly Dog Father,

Odinn: I have been a good Jewish boy and I want to thank you, Heavenly Dog Father, for giving us wonderful parents who love us and take us hiking and exploring. Always protect them and bless them.
Frigga, have you anything to add?

Frigga: Well, Odinn as you know I am an Agnostic Lutheran, so I guess if the Heavenly Dog Father can help us get off this and find our way back to the trail, I would put that on the positive column and go from there.

"Trails Are Us,
Frigga and Odinn

My Dad

For: Jim Dovel

Dear Heavenly Dog Father,

I miss my dad. he never knew how sick I was! He used to scratch my back and talk to me like I could understand him, which I could, you know. You taught us all how to understand our parents. I remember when Dad and Mom first adopted me after the fire. My previous Mom and Dad left their house to get away from the fire and didn't take me, so I ran. My new Dad trusted me right away. I didn't know that so I ran, and Dad came after me! He really wanted me back. He told if I came to my new home he would give me a snack. I followed him home and never left again. My friend Buddy in South Dakota said my Dad was really sad when he knew I died. I asked Buddy to help and I saw he did a really good job!

If I ever get to have new parents again I hope I can have the same ones again!

Love,
Buddy

The Best Daddy In The World

For: Matt DeMeyer

Dear Heavenly Dog Father,

I want to give love and thanks to my dad for loving me, taking care of my daily needs like my ear infections, cleaning out my eye goobers, the delicious variety of treats and feeding me my healthy food that keep me fit and live longer!!!

But I could suggest that he could give me more than two daily walks! Two is simply not enough. Well at least I am not trapped in a kennel. LOL!

Your loving companion,
Miss Jenny

"Well at least I am not trapped in a kennel. LOL!"

A Prayer From A Shelter Dog

For: Thalía Arenas

(My poem is complete...)
Prayer from an adopted shelter dog...

Dear Heavenly Dog Father,

Guard my friend, keeper and mother. For she is my
companion, partner and mate. She saved me from a terrible
fate. So I love her unconditionally. With loyalty and
consistency. For she may have many flaws, But my heart
knows no other law, than to love her forever, regardless of
her endeavors. Because of her, I am alive. And ever since
she is mine. She calls me dog. I call her mom. No better
words to describe the love I feel as I recite a prayer tonight.

Thoughtfully,
Just A Shelter dog

My First Picture

For: Alexander Dumonde

Dear Heavenly Dog Father,

I know this is a lot to take in at 8 weeks old and on my first day in your new home, but Odinn my new parents wanted me to know that they will love me and do whatever they can to make me a happy dog.

They named me Odinn Agape because they said that I was the epitome of unconditional love. I am pretending to understand them. Or maybe I just need to pee?

Love,
Odinn

" ...they said that I was the epitome of unconditional love."

My Gorgeous Six Pack

For: Coral Biller

Dear Heavenly Dog Father,

The 6 of us are coming to you to say THANK YOU for giving us the family we have! We are so loved and adored by our family that we know it and feel it every second of every day!

Thank You Heavenly Dog Father.

Love,
The Very Appreciative Biller 6 Pack

" We are so loved and adored by our family."

So Grateful

For: Roger Reyes

Dear Heavenly Dog Father,

I thank you Heavenly Dog Father for blessing me with such a loving home and a master who adores me. I know there were other dogs before me. I feel so grateful to have replaced them after they crossed the rainbow bridge. My wish is to fill my owner's life with love and joy every single day!

Thank you!
Shadow

Hey it's Stella!

For: Steve Ronce

Dear Heavenly Dog Father,

My name is Stella. I'm a Great Dane. I just wanted to thank the Heavenly Dog Father for my Master here on Earth. He takes care of all my needs. I just wish all dogs had homes and a Master like me. And when my Master is sad, I comfort him! It's a Perfect Relationship.

Thank you Heavenly Father for all I have! Amen.

Love,
Stella

For Goodness Sakes Take A Bath!

For: John Humphrey

Dear Heavenly Dog Father,

You know I simply can't go on a walk with my owner until he shampoos his hair. Or I will be too embarrassed to be seen with him!

And while you're at it can you add a few more fire hydrants in front of my house?

Love,
Darth

"And while you're at it can you add a few more fire hydrants in front of my house?"

My Brothers And Sisters

For: Laura Mullins

Hello there my Heavenly Dog Father,

I'm talking to you again. Please bless my home and family. I'm really praying hard for all my brothers and sisters that are in rescues or shelters to make sure they get a good home like me! With plenty of hugs, kisses, fantastic food and SLEEPING IN BED! I really thank you for finding me this family, and this is me signing off. Amen.

Love,
Angel

"I'm really praying hard for all my brothers and sisters that are in rescues or shelters...."

A New Pair Of Eyes

For: Michael Zentner

Dear Heavenly Dog Father,

My owner has an eye problem. He will most likely go blind sometime and won't be able to see me. He doesn't talk about it much, but I know he worries a bit. That being stated, he seems to still want to play with me and take our walks. I think he knows how short our time is on this pile of dirt, and decided he will live every moment no matter what happens to him or me.

I will help him by rolling in all kinds of stuff so he can smell me wherever I am. I can also bring him things he can't find, especially the stuff I took and buried cause I wuv him so.

If you could bring him some new eyes that would be nice! Even if you don't, rest assured I will be here to take care of him as he has taken care of me for so very long. It's the least I can do.

Love And Kisses
BeBe Dog.

All That Is And All That Isn't

For: Nancy Priestly

Dear Heavenly Dog Father,

I have been so blessed to spend time with my beloved companion, Nancy Priestly!

This is the second life we have spent together. The first life was in Texas when I went by the name of Moglie as a Blue Doberman.

We spent 12 wonderful years together in that life, and I was part of an extraordinary Doberman Family of 5. We Dobermans were able to sit at the dining room table on chairs to eat. After dinner, the five of us Dobie's would sit on the bed with Nancy and she would put video dog movies on the TV's for us.

Nancy would take us in the van to pick up food and we would go on an adventure to run to the park and eat lunch on a picnic bench. We ate so well and she would make us Doggie Nutrition Bars.

Because of our deep love and understanding of each other I wanted to come back again to be with Nancy. I was hoping she would recognize me and we could continue our enjoyment of life together.

It was such a beautiful life! I wanted to come back and be with her. So I came back as a min-pin which looks like a shrunk down version of a Doberman. In the beginning, she had a bit of a resistance since she had just lost my two sisters and felt she didn't have room in her heart for a new addition.

However, it didn't take long until she opened her heart. Eventually recognized that is was me, Moglie once again, who had come back to her as Max. She recognized the love and energy that I was. So we spent another 15 years together.

I hope and pray that Nancy has a wonderful life, and I am watching over her. She does know this and talks to me on the other side from time to time. My love for her is outside of time and space, and she is aware of that.

Someday, maybe if things line up I will come back to her again in this life of hers for a third time. Who knows?? Our love for each other is not diminished, and is forever with beautiful memories along the way.

Love, Max

To My Beloved Max

For: Max Priestly

Dear Heavenly Dog Father,

This is my prayer to Max, my love, who is now a centurion in doggie years. 7 years to our one year and he is 15 years old. A beautiful Min Pin Chihuahua mix.

Fifteen years ago I was coming out of a real estate office in Fallbrook and a woman approached me and had small puppy inside a plastic bag, and it looked half dead. He pushed bag in my hand and spoke in a language that is foreign to me. I said no, since I was still grieving from the loss of my Doberman. I didn't feel my heart was ready to embrace a new puppy yet. Another person came over and said to me that the woman wants me to have this dog. Yet another person arrived and said I was to take the dog. Not thinking clearly, I took the plastic bag with the half dead puppy in it, to see if I could revive it. I took it to my son's home and worked with it to see if it would revive. I gave it water and loved it up. I told my son I couldn't keep the dog and asked him to take it for the time being. So as the story usually goes, I fell in love with the puppy and he did revive. We have been through much together life and death experiences, and now Max is 100 years old in doggie years. So this is what I have written to him.

Our time together is stored in a chamber of my heart. Remembering the love, the joy, the happiness, and the beautiful sadness of our precious moments together. Looking into his beautiful eyes. A pause a moment of stillness where the universe is revealed. Thank you Max for our journey together. There is not time, but our life is timeless, Outside of time and space, more than these magnificent bodies that we have in place.

I love you Max forever!

Love, Nancy Priestly

Walkies?

For: Angela Smallwood

Dear Heavenly Dog Father,

My Mommy Angela would take me on a morning walk. We would end our walk with me running around. And then I would round up the geese. I would put them in a circle and run right though the middle. I miss that time!

Love,
AJ (Andrew Jackson)

"My Mommy took me on morning walks...."

My Little AJ (Andrew Jackson)

For: Angela Smallwood

Dear Heavenly Dog Father,

My little A J, I wish up on a star. I hope you are in heaven with your partner, my father. Dad loved the story about you when you were younger.

Love,
Angela Smallwood

P.S. My father fell in love with A J. When I sent the story to you I was thinking about both of them up in heaven together. I miss both of them very much.

Just wanted to let you know why I sent it to you.

Petey and Mommies Dreams

For: Alyssa F.

Dear Heavenly Dog Father,

    As I lay down in my slumber to sleep, I dream of the dogs I wish we could keep. White, brown, black, chestnut and red. So many cuties that run through mommies head. We pray that we give them a place to run graceful and free.

    We would then see how truly happy they'd be, love, cuddles and so much affection with us. All doggies need a best friend without an exception Mommy and I pray all the doggies are cozy tonight. As I lay down I hold my own Mommy tight!

My Love,
Petey

"I dream of the dogs I wish we could keep."

Prayer Against Doggage

For: Victor Bermeo C.

Give Us, Oh Heavenly Dog Father,

A Sensitive Heart to fight against abuse dogs. It is very shameful that neither Preachers nor Moralists raise their voice against of Dog Abuse. You who created them to keep us company in this life.

For the Love that I profess, I ask you to help me by giving me the necessary strength to help my master and his family to fight against this Injustice and to make man have mercy on all Living Creatures since that will be Noble.

Dear Heavenly Dog Father, I place all my hopes on you. Amen.

In Gratitude,
Greysi

Take Care Of The Doggies

For: Laura Lyons

Dear Heavenly Dog Father,

I want to thank you for my Mommy and Daddy. They said I rescued them, but they indeed rescued me from a monster that was way too mean to me in the first 3 months of my life. When my Mommy took me into a room at the shelter where the monster dumped me, I was so scared and she was full of love. I could not have asked for a better Mommy. I was truly blessed when they walked in and saw me. I know my Mommy was leery, because I was really scared, really thin, and she tossed a toy to me and all I wanted to do was run out of the room, I was horrified when the toy came towards me. When she saw how scared I was, I thought for sure I was going back to my cage, but instead she got tears in her eyes and told me "she and Daddy would never hurt me." I sniffed the toy and walked towards my new Mommy and sniffed her hand and it was pure love. I crawled up in her lap and lay down. I wanted to go home with them so bad. When I left I rode home on Mommy's lap.

When we pulled up in the driveway and got out, I saw steps and began to shake because I had been kicked and thrown down steps at my previous home. My Mommy picked me up and carried me in the house. They put fresh food and water out for me, but I was too scared to eat or drink because my previous owner had kicked me and beat me over food, so I would grab a mouthful of food and run into a room where nobody was and woof it down. These people really shocked me because they were really nice to me and gave me all kinds of toys, and lots of love. My

Mommy took me on long walks.

I want to thank You, Heavenly Dog Father, for giving me the best Mommy in the world. She is still awesome with me even though I am old now. They adopted me at 3 months old and I am now 14 yrs. old and they still love me and always will love me. I would like to ask you to give me many more years with them because they are the best, and when I leave them I know they will be sad for a long time.

Thank you Heavenly Dog Father for bringing us all together as a family. My Mommy gave up a lot for me and I know I am in the best place I could ever be and want to stay here with them as long as I can. I see my Mommy cry when I don't feel good, and I know she is worried about me leaving her too soon, so please, Heavenly Dog Father, all I ask is for more time with them, and I thank You for bringing them into my life. They say I rescued them, but indeed they rescued me. I guess we rescued each other. Thank You, Heavenly Dog Father. I pray this in your name. AMEN.

Love,
Baby

Just A Silly Poodle

For: Elise Bell and Imani

Dear Heavenly Dog Father,

You already know me. I am Markie, a cute little poodle, and my owners are Elise and her son, Imani. I pray that my owner Elise accomplishes her goals and is successful in attracting wealth and good karma. I pray that Imani graduates with his Associates degree and transfers to UC Davis next year. I pray for myself to keep eating that delicious organic dog food and to have Elise and Imani in my life for a long time.

Kisses to you,
Markie

A Doggies Prayer

For: Crystal Davis And All Dogs

Dear Heavenly Dog Father,

Our Father who art in heaven, hallowed be thy name.

I pray for my previous owners who had to give me up for adoption.

Give them peace Lord, knowing I have been rescued by an amazing family.

Bless them Lord that one day they will find another best friend as great as me.

I also want to pray for my new family.

I pray that you continue to bless them in more ways than they can imagine.

I know I am here not by chance but by your grace and mercy.

Blessing them Lord,

For obeying you,

And thank you for adopting me.

In the Heavenly Dog Fathers name I pray. Amen!

All Dogs

Paws In Prayer

For: Morgan Hartt

Dear Heavenly Dog Father,

We join in prayer for our master...

In the deep and dark nights of the soul,

When the world seems darker...

When you fear you just can't make it...

We understand;

We will lick your face.

Wait for pets. And let you know the world is not quite so dark.

Please protect and bless us, our master, and our home.

This we pray and we give thanks...

Signed,
Emma Louise

Treat Me Kindly

For: Eddie Illiescu

Dear Heavenly Dog Father,

Treat me kindly, my beloved master, for no heart in the entire world is more grateful for kindness there loving heart of me. When it's cold and wet, please take me inside, for I am now a domesticated animal no longer use to bitter elements, I ask for no greater glory then the privilege of sitting by your feet beside the hearth....

Lovingly,
Luna, Lino

From: Eddie Illiescu...

O Lord Jesus Christ, our Savior, Physician of all living things, who through Thy love and compassion doth heal all manner of sickness and affliction: do thou O Lord visit this pet Luna and Lino of his and her health and happiness.

Love & Light & Oneness

For: Rev. Dr. Vickie Fothen

Dear Heavenly Dog Father, The One Holy God of all,

I pray this prayer for everybody, every child, every animal. We were put on this earth in the image of God to take care of it, according to Genesis in the Bible. We look to our hearts where God is in each and every one of us to help those who suffer in any way we can even, if it is a phone call. God is thanking you for your kindness.

Thank God for all the animal rescuers all over the world who bring animals to safe secure places and for those who take a rescue animal into their care. Allowing sick animals to stay in a safe place keeping them company letting them lick your face. Telling these animals they will be okay; we got you now. You are a blessing and you make a difference not only in the animal you help but in your own life and others as well. The world sees you all as heroes that you are. God sees you as His lights! Thank you, Father, for your lights.

In Christ Spirit, Amen.
Milly

My Mom's Divine Ministry

For: Sharon Jackson

Dear Heavenly Dog Father,

My name is God's Amazing Grace. I'm called Grace for short.

I'm asking for prayers for my friend - to the south, east, west and the north,

I follow her around daily as she works in her calling to help others.

To many of these girls/women, she is their only mother...

Her ministry is her deep and devoted thought, now and from the start.

God, please give her the desires of her heart,

It seems that the odds are against the desires she has for the ministry to grow.

Her trust in God, for He has the power and the end. He has the know....

When she accepted Jesus and was saved from her sins,

I know you have a plan for my special friend...

Sending Kisses,
Amazing Grace

The Barbeque

For: Alexander Dumonde

Dear Heavenly Dog Father,

I hope that my parents are making one of those steaks in the barbecue for us, let it be succulent, medium rare, and ...

Frigga: Excuse me Odinn but haven't you anything better for which to pray than just a steak?

Odinn: I am sorry. You are right. Dear Heavenly Dog Father, let us also have a side of potatoes and brussel sprouts. Amen!

Wishfully thinking,
Odinn and Frigga

Divine Healing

For: Bnai T Madden

Dear Heavenly Dog Father,

We are Snoop 'n' Bear. We're praying to you for our mom Bnai. She's sick and not doing so well. We want her to get better so she can take care of us. Amen.

Love,
Snoop 'n' Bear

"We want her to get better so she can take care of us."

Dog's Prayer To Our Heavenly Dog Father

For: Ruphas Resupas

Dear Heavenly Dog Father,

I come before you saying thank you for the gift of life and for giving me a wonderful ally. I pray that you bless the home of my friend so that even my living can be improved. I pray that you bless him with more money so that I can improve my living standards also. I pray that you bless my owner with a good health so that we can live long as a family. I pray that you give us a good relationship and good understanding where we can play and enjoy ourselves forever.

Heavenly Dog Father, I pray that you're going to bless him with a willing heart to teach me more skills so that I can outdo my other friends.

Please also bless my owner with a ship so that we can be enjoying the view of the ocean and swimming in deep waters of the ocean. If you bless him with all these, all the glory will be unto you.

I also pray that you'll bless him with a big house so that I can get my own room and have the best meals! This I pray trusting in the name of the Heavenly Dog Father and the Holy Spirit. Amen.

Love,
Galan

Our Blessed Memories

For: Tammy King

Ok Kojack and Spike would say

Dear Heavenly Dog Father,

Mom, we miss you and love woo you. What an amazing mama we had!

We loved playing together and hanging out and just sleeping with you.

Spike and I and mama snuggled up with each other. Loving each other everyday and being there for each other! What a great gift we had, just the three of us.

Sending you our love,
Kojack and Spike

P.S. I miss them everyday and always are with me.

My Best Friend Barkley

For: Rebecca Atkins (Beckie)

Dear Heavenly Dog Father,

HEAVENLY FATHER Plzzzz DON'T TAKE MY MOM. I WAITED FOR MY KIND MOMMIE FOR FOREVER. I'M NEVER WITHOUT LOTS OF HUGS. SHE LOVES ME SOOO MUCH. SHE KNOWS I WORRY ABOUT HER.

Lots Of Hugs,
Barkley Atkinson

ALL HER FRIENDS LOVE ME. THEY SEE HOW MUCH I LOVE HER AND SHE LOVES ME SOOOOOOOOOOOOOOOOOOOOOOOOOOOOOO PLZ PLZ PLX HEAVENLY FATHER HEAL HER IN JESUS NAME!!!!!!!!!!!!!!!!!!!!!!!!!

PS BARKLEY AND I ARE MIRACLES. I PRAYED FOR HIM FOR 2 OR 3 YEARS. DIDN'T HAVE ANY CLUE I WAS GONNA GET HIM. MY FRIEND AND I WERE WALKING AROUND AND SHE ASKED ME IF I WANTED TO LOOK AROUND IN PETSMART AND I SAID YEAH. NOT KNOWING THERE WERE ADOPTIONS, WE WENT IN AND PRETTY SURE HE SAW ME FIRST!

BECAUSE WHEN I DID SEE HIM, HE WAS ALREADY STARING AT ME. WE COULDN'T TAKE OUR EYES OFF OF EACH OTHER. BUT I'M NOT OLD, NOT RICH AND LIVED IN AN APT. A LADY SAW OUR INTERACTION AND SAID U HAVE TO HAVE THIS DOG. I SAID I WANT HIM REAL BAD BUT I LIVE IN AN APT. SHE DIDN'T TAKE NO FOR AN ANSWER.. PRAISE GOD! I KNOW GOD PUT US TOGETHER BECAUSE HE IS ME WITH FUR. HE'S SUPER SUPER SMART!!!!!!!!!!!!! HE'S MY BFF

OHhhh. A PRAYER FOR GOD TO LET ME LIVE LONGER CAUSE I WANT BARKLEY TO NEVER BE DEPRESSED, AND WE AND THEY CAN DIE FROM A BROKEN HEART LITERALLY.

Humans Are The Best!

For: Amber Cohen-Havranek

Dear Heavenly Dog Father,

Our hoomans are the best! They never get upset when we put all our toys in the bed with us. Or when my brother gives his ball a drink of water and puts water all over the kitchen floor! Or when we chase the cat to play, or when we get a new toy, we tear the stuffin out of it. Or miss the pad and tinkle on the floor.

We are blessed! Please keep them safe like they keep us safe. We love them just as much as they love us. Amen.

With lots of joy!
Rocky and Tippy

My Three Dogs

For: Linda M. Lukas

Dear Heavenly Dog Father,

I love you. Please stand by my owner in the same way she stands by me! Jesus, I have only one short life. Let me make it a great life.

Love your crew,
Taylor, Thallia (Shorty) and Cali.....

"Please stand by my owner in the same way she stands by me!"

The Rainbow Bridge

For: Esmee Cope

Dear Heavenly Dog Father,

Can you grant me a wish?
I want my mummy to come 'n' pick me up from the rainbow bridge to take me to my favorite place, the park. I loved playing with my football. I also killed tennis balls 'n' running around with my furry friends.

Love, Delilah

P.S. I just want my lil lady back n back in my arms n' her sloppy kisses on mummy's face 'n' her crazy bark miss all that. xxxxx

My Love For You Is All Around

For: Jasper's Mum

Dear Heavenly Dog Father,

I send a prayer for my human dog mum. I have been so loved and treated like a son since I came into my forever family's home. My mum adores me, and when she is sad I always know when to kiss and lay on her lap for cuddles. There's been so much that my mum has gone through, and yet she always smiles though it all .We have a special mother and son bond and I love her lots, also not forgetting my dad and human brother.

Licks and paws,
Jasper

Our Dog Father

For: Saundra Hutchinson

Dear Heavenly Dog Father,

Heavenly Dog Father are you there?
Please show a sign we're in your care.
You created us and called us a dog
Unbeknownst to humans we're their god.
Here on earth we frolic and play
Amazing everyone in our special way,
Along the way we might chew a shoe,
Unfortunately that's what we sometimes do,
Because we love our humans very much
We're rewarded by cuddles a loving touch
We are on earth for such a short time
In a loving home until we reach our prime.
Oh Heavenly Dog Father, when we come home
We leave our humans here all alone.
Will you reach out your hand from above
Spread your arms around the ones we love
They'll be upset because we aren't there
Whilst we frolic and play again in your loving care.

Love,
Toby

Guardian Angel

For: Israel Magdaleno

Dear Heavenly Dog Father,

Please make my daddy, Israel, feel all better. He's been sick way too long. To cheer him up, his beloved girlfriend, Wendy bought him a shiny new car for Christmas. She wanted to give him hope and a reason to live.

I get worried when I see strange tubes in his body. It seems like he has some new ones.

I lie on his bed every night as his guardian angel. I want to make sure he is sleeping safe and sound. I want to protect him. I want to cure him.

Heavenly Dog Father can you with your amazing grace help heal him?

Lovingly,
Cowboy

P.S. He got a transplant and is doing great!

Our Special Times

For: CC Coltrain

Dear Heavenly Dog Father,

Please watch over my human, CC. She works too hard and doesn't give me enough treats! Please help her figure out how to spend more time with me because she laughs a lot more when she does — and I love belly rubs, and they take time! Bless her for feeding me, taking me outside, letting me sniff every tree and post and mailbox in the neighborhood, and, oh yeah, rubbing my belly. She is an angel so watch out for her!

Thank You,
Lucy (Dona Clara Lucia)

"Please help my human figure out how to spend more time with me."

Thankfulness For My Life

For: The Marsh Family

Dear Heavenly Dog Father,

Oh, Heavenly Dog Father I have some thoughts and observations that I wanted to share with you. I don't feel that I've changed over the last 10 years, maybe a few more white whiskers, and a slightly larger belly, but my family has seen so many changes that it's hard to keep up. We've gone from a house of three, where I was the star of the show, to a house of 5, where these two little girls run the show. It used to be so easy for me to find my dog toys; now I must sift through princess dresses, markers, fake food that doesn't smell but looks so good, and all these stuffed animals that look like mine. But I'm not complaining at all; it just has been different. I used to be watched like a hawk by the adults whenever I'd get close to a table or counter with food on it, but now they're so focused on those girls that it's like taking candy from a baby. I can slowly walk up, wait for the adults to be distracted by whatever the girls are doing and then, bam, I can quickly pop up, get a few bites, and lay down like nothing happened. The girls also leave a trail of crumbs in their wake that I feel it's better I get than the vacuum cleaner. I guess some of this might explain my slightly larger belly, but kids' scraps are so delicious.

With all the change, there's one thing that's stayed the same, and that's the need for me to protect the family and house from all the dangers. And I thank you for giving me that strength to constantly protect even when I'm completely exhausted. My family has no idea how many times there've been close calls and I've saved their lives. I hear every rumble of a motorcycle, every squeak of a wheel turning around in the cul-de-sac, and most importantly EVERY single delivery truck that comes down this street (and there are SO many of those trucks!!). Speaking of delivery trucks, there's this thing called Amazon, and 10 years ago I never saw any

Amazon trucks or people come to the door, but now it's like they're trying to take over the house. And the really tough part, is that they don't always come in a truck that says "Amazon," so I really have to step up my game and make sure I'm protecting against ALL vans and sometimes even cars!! These truck drivers sometimes even have the nerve to come up to our front porch! But thanks to your strength, I always hear them before they get to the door and I sprint right to the front window by the door, raise the hackles, show them my teeth, claw at the blinds, fog up the window with my breath, and yell at them so loudly "This is my house stranger, I'm protecting this house and you are not welcome!!!!". They never get in no matter how hard they try (or don't try), and they always are so scared that they drop the package in their hands, run away frantically with their "tails" between their legs, and race away in the truck they drove up in all thanks to me! Sure, there's some blind and drywall damage but that's a small price to pay for home safety. There's just so many of these Amazon, UPS, and FedEx trucks that even in the car or on walks I'm just constantly protecting the family from these dangers. I know my family really appreciates my barking because every time I start barking, they cheer me on by yelling my name, "Hayden!", giving me more motivation to keep barking even louder.

Oh there's something else I wanted to say but I can't remember…Oh yeah the birds, there's just something not right about how they can taunt me when they're standing on the ground and then just fly away when I come over to play. One of these days I'll get one of those pesky birds like I've gotten the lizards, rabbits, and rats!

Heavenly Dog Father, I wanted to just let you know how things have changed over the last 10 years and how some things just have always stayed the same. But I know my place and I've stayed true to my role these past 10 years, thank you!

Thank You,
Hayden Marsh

Do You Know How Much I Love You?

To: Gunner & Ken Fraser

To Gunner, (my dog)

Do you know how much I love you?
Even though you sometimes piddle on the legs of the furniture,
Do you know how much I love you?
Even though it is so embarrassing when you bark like a crazed lunatic at the neighbors,
Do you know how much I love you?
Even though you rip out all the stuffing from your pillows and make a mess,
Do you know how much I love you?
Even though when I leave you in the house by yourself you howl like your being tortured,
Do you know how much I love you?*...very, very much!!!*

Thank you Heavenly Dog Father for giving me Gunner.

To Ken, (my human)

Do you know how much I love you?
Even though you scold me for <u>sometimes</u> piddling on the legs of the furniture,
Do you know how much I love you?
Even though you get upset with me when I bark and try to protect you from the neighbors, other dogs, squirrels...,
Do you know how much I love you?
Even though you can't understand that pillow stuffing is evil and must go,
Do you know how much I love you?
Even though you leave me in this big scary house all by myself,
Do you know how much I love you?*...very, very much!!!*

Thank you Heavenly Dog Father for giving me my human.

Written by Ken Fraser, owner of Gunner Blue, an adorable miniature Dachshund

A Conversational Prayer With Bella and Her Heavenly Dog Father

To: Frederick Evans

Bella: Dear Heavenly Dog Father this is Bella!

Heavenly Dog Father: Yes, Bella I hear you.

Bella: I wanted to report to you!

Heavenly Dog Father: Speak!

Bella: I am so happy and grateful. I worry about my master. He still cries over Rio, my brother. So I go to him and tell him everything is wonderful. That Rio is playing like he used to.

Heavenly Dog Father: Oh, yes Bella my beautiful one. He is still entertaining here as he did there. He knocks over the big bucket of water and carries it by the handle as he….

Bella: He prances over to the baby pool then plops in it! Then he…

Heavenly Dog Father: He gets all the toys from all over the park and puts them in the pool. Then he gets the hose nozzle in his mouth and drags it over in the pool.

Bella: And then he tells our human master to turn the water on! Woof! And everyone laughs and cheers. Oh what a joyful time!

Heavenly Dog Father: Your human master could not have given you better names for my Rio loves the water and my Bella is so beautiful!

Bella: Woof! Woof!

Heavenly Dog Father: And Bella, keep up the good work! I will speak with you soon!

Love,

Bella: Woof! Woof! Woof!

Moms Cause

For: Shelby Pierce

Dear Heavenly Dog Father,

God, please help my mom help all the little "doxies" that can't help themselves. Give her the inspiration to keep making her "doxie" creations that make so many people happy and help our furry friends. Help heal her heart for the loss of her other fur baby, Munchkin, and keep her safe. Amen.

Love,
Dee

"Please help my mom help all the little 'doxies' that can't help themselves."

We Ask You To Bless Us

For: Jill Sheu

Dear Heavenly Dog Father,

Please bless us. She's my best friend, my partner, my defender, my Mom. I will be faithful and true until the last beat of my heart; we're a bonded and dedicated pair, my Mom and me.

Forever Yours,
Darci

To My Best Friend Darci from your Mama (Jill)

A Prayer for Animals –Albert Schweitzer Hear our humble prayer, O God, for our friends the animals, especially for animals who are suffering; for any that are hunted or lost or deserted or frightened or hungry; for all that must be put to death. We entreat for them all Thy mercy and pity, and for those who deal with them, we ask a heart of compassion and gentle hands and kindly words. Make us, ourselves, to be true friends to animals and so to share the blessings of the merciful.

P.S. It really says what I feel. Let me know.

Prayer From Russy In Heaven To Shani On Earth

For: Shani Jinaki

Dear Heavenly Dog Father,

I was lost and found on a man's doorstep.
He had three cats bigger than me!
I lost my home and God eventually gave me a home with you.
One of those first evenings, when the thunder boomed, I jumped in your lap and you held me tight until I stopped shaking. Right then I knew I was safe with you.

What I didn't know is how I would make you feel safe with me. I didn't know how PTSD debilitated you. Before I arrived, it kept you in the house hiding from the stimulation of the world outside your door. And then you were forced to walk me regularly. That alone changed your world for the better. Then, in came my stylish and comfortable travel bag. You took me everywhere with you. We even went places that don't allow dogs and they accepted me. I was your baby. But of course, the rules bowed down to me! I'm just too adorable for words.

I'm so glad I made you feel safe to come out of the shell that was holding you back in life. I'm glad to look down on you growing even more into yourself and growing stronger and better.

With you, I went from being a stray dog to being your emotional support dog that eased PTSD symptoms. I believe I showed you how to live and care again. Maybe you love my furry kind too much, Shani. Give some of that love you have for us dogs to some humans. It's okay. Don't worry. God will protect you like He did me and placed me with you. God will put the right and safe people in your life. I'm glad to have warmed your heart up, Shani

I love you. I miss you. I am waiting to see you again, Shani.

Love,
Russy

A Glimpse Of Heaven

For: Sean Sill

Dear Heavenly Dog Father,

Hi too! My dad and I are best friends on earth and eventually when we get to heaven. He is my human soul mate. I promise you. When I pass on, my dog soul will wait for your soul. And we will to become one once again.

No longer in the form that I was while on earth, but different. And I will wait at the rainbow bridge to wag my tail once more once I see your smiling face.

All for my love for you my dad,
Love Max

P.S. Yes Max am still thinking one from me. How I feel is I know he has aged and I think he's not got too long… But the first day he jumped on my knee all those years ago I know we had some thing special.

I think he was sent to me from my daughter I lost. I've always felt she had something to do with it. I did not really know the love Max and I had and have. If I was a dog, I would be him. And if Max was human, he would be me.

We do not have to say anything because we just know each other so well! It's hard to explain. I have never loved anything in life more than Max and am not ashamed to say it! But the bond we have would never be broken. It's heaven now for us. And when he's gone, that's when it will feel like hell. Thank you, Lara. It means so much to me and Max for you asking me and so proud thank you.

Heavenly Dog Father

Heavenly Dog Father
Thank you for my birth
Upon planet earth
I'm dancing in mirth

Heavenly Dog Father
Thank you for mom
She so nice and calm
Reads to me a psalm

Heavenly Dog Father
I so love my home
Food water and a comb
Land I get to roam

Heavenly Dog Father
I'm adored lots here
There's nothing to fear
My name is Shakespeare

Heavenly Dog Father
You've made me happy
I've got a family
Ev'ryone loves me

Love,
Shakespeare
@Ladee Bassett

My Name Is Peanut

For: Esther Marie Wells

Dear Heavenly Dog Father,

My name is Peanut and I crossed the Rainbow Bridge
a little over a year and a half ago. My life was rather
cut short due to a freak accident. And my Mommy still
cries about it to this day. But she doesn't need to cry she
knows she'll see me again and that I think her everyday
for saving me from what she called a hoarder. I just know
there were tons of other dogs including my own sons
and everybody had to go to a new home and nobody had
chosen me. Everybody wanted my boys because they
were so tiny but nobody looked at me. Then one day in
walked my Mommy. Of course I didn't know it at the
time I was really shy wouldn't go up to anybody. But she
picked me up put me on her lap. I wouldn't even look at
her, nor give her a kiss but she said this one's for me. So
we went on a long trip and ended up at Mommy's house.
I was on my Best Manners ever. The other lady calls my
Mommy that I wasn't potty-trained. But that wasn't true
I wasn't allowed to go outside so as soon as Mommy
brought me home I did my business and her little yard.
At first she kept the leash on me but then she used to drop
it and I stayed right by her side. She's a dog trainer and
she always told me I was the best little girl ever. I didn't
always like to wear a dress, but if you put one on me,
I sure liked the attention that I got for those frilly little
dresses. Little kid's love me, anybody who met me seems

to love me and that's all because I was shown the people are good and they want to treat their pets like family. So thank you dear Heavenly Dog Father for allowing me share three wonderful years with my Mommy. I'm waiting here for her everyday and I can't wait to see her again because she loves me so much and I miss her. Heavenly Dog Father I know my Mommy praises you. She had me so in her prayers please relieve some of her pain over the loss of me. I'm up here with my one of my sisters. She lived to be 18 and a half so Mommy was really sad when she left but I know she really misses me. Thank you Heavenly Dog Father for taking the time listen to me.

Love,
Peanut

Arriverò Nala

Perché quando ve ne andate ci strappate l'anima?
Cosa avete voi anime belle che noi umani non potremo
mai capire? Vi guardo e siete così belli e vi penso sempre
così anche quando siete sul Ponte. Gesù ti prego prenditi
cura di loro gioca con loro così come facevano quando
erano con noi. Il dolore che mi prende ogni volta che uno
di voi se ne va è un dolore cannibale mi mangia dentro
mi lascia senza fiato a volte odio il momento in cui il
mio cuore ha iniziato ad amarvi. Potrei scrivere un fiume
di parole ma nessuna può esprimere il vuoto che sento
dentro di me. Ora vi saluto non voglio disturbare il vostro
gioco lassù e se me lo sono meritato aspettatemi quando
sarà il mio momento vorrei tuffarmi in mezzo a voi.

—Romano Quattropanetti

I'll Get Nala

Because when you leave
Do you tear our souls out?
What do you have, beautiful souls
That we humans will never understand?
I look at you and you're so beautiful
And I always think of you like this,
Even when you're on the bridge.
Jesus please take care of them
Play with them
Just as they did
When they were with us.
The pain that takes me
Every time one of you leaves,
It's a cannibal pain
Eats me in.
It leaves me breathless
Sometimes I hate the moment
Where my heart
Began to love you.
I could write a river of words
But none can express
The emptiness I feel inside me.
Now I greet you
I don't want to disturb your game
There
And I deserved it
Wait
When it's my time
I'd like to dive among you.

—Romano Quattropanetti

"If you find it in your heart to care for somebody else, you will have succeeded."

—Maya Angelou

Other Books by Lara Magallon

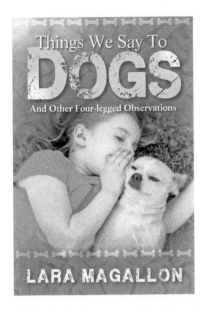

Things We Say To Dogs

Dogs. Faithful and true, mans best friend and companion to the end. We treat them like family, and so they are. Have you ever had a conversation with your furry friend? Sure you have! In this extremely whimsical, delightful book you will stumble across some kooky comments and observations about dogs not only from me, but others. If you're a dog lover you will definitely relate to this fun filled book.

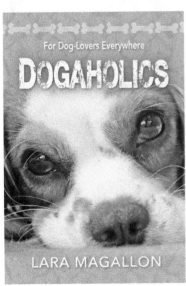

Dogaholics

Have you ever stayed up at night wondering what exactly your dog thinks about you?

What would they say if they could talk?

Or if they have crossed over the "rainbow bridge" to join the "Heavenly Dog Father" and his "Dog Angels," are they still watching over us?

Is there another side of life where all dogs both past and present exist?

If you are attempting to unlock the mysteries of our beloved canine companions, then "DogAholics" is meant for you!

CPSIA information can be obtained
at www.ICGtesting.com
Printed in the USA
FSHW021724281021
85724FS